Bernard-

ROBERTO ZUCCO

Methuen Drama

Bernard-Marie Koltès

Roberto Zucco

Translated by Martin Crimp

Methuen Drama

Published by Methuen

2 4 6 8 10 9 7 5 3 1

Copyright 1990 Les Editions de Minuit

Translation copyright © 1997 by Martin Crimp

Endnote extracts copyright © 1997 by Pascale Froment,
extracts from the work of Bernard-Marie Koltès copyright
© Les Editions de Minuit, John Freeman's 'Face to Face'
interview reproduced by kind permission of BBC Worldwide

Chronology copyright © 1997 by David Bradby

The authors and translator have asserted their moral rights.

First published in the United Kingdom in 1997 by
Methuen Drama, Random House, 20 Vauxhall Bridge Road,
London SW1V 2SA

Random House UK Limited Reg. No. 954009

A CIP catalogue record for this book
is available fom the British Library

ISBN 0 413 73080 8

Typeset from Author's disc by
MATS, Southend-on-Sea, Essex
Printed and bound in Great Britain by
Cox & Wyman Ltd, Reading, Berkshire

Caution

Bernard-Marie Koltès:
Chronology

1948 Birth of Bernard-Marie Koltès (9 April) at Metz, a town in the Eastern part of France. His father, a professional soldier, was away in Algeria for much of the 1950s.

1958-62 Koltès's secondary schooling began against a background of bombings and disturbances as the crisis of the Algerian conflict pushed France to the brink of civil war.

1967 After completing school in Metz, Koltès went to Strasbourg, where he attended courses at the School of Journalism. He also studied music, and even considered becoming a professional organist.

1968 In January he saw Maria Casarès, at Strasbourg, playing the central role in Seneca's *Medea*; this was his first visit to a theatre and had an profound effect on him. During the May 1968 occupations of colleges and factories Koltès avoided political involvement. In the Summer he travelled to Paris, and then to New York.

1969 First attempt at writing for the theatre: a stage adaptation of Gorki's *My Childhood*, entitled *Les Amertumes [Bitternesses]*; he sent the play to Hubert Gignoux, director of the Strasbourg National Drama School, asking for advice.

1970 Koltès directed a few friends in a production of his play at the Théâtre du Quai, Strasbourg (performances in May and June). Hubert Gignoux saw the production and invited Koltès to join his course in the *régie* (technical) section of the School. He joined, but dropped out during his second year.

1971 He wrote and directed his second and third plays in the same little student Théâtre du Quai: *La Marche [The March]*, based on the Song of Songs, and *Procès Ivre [Drunken Trial]*, based on Dostoyevski's *Crime and Punishment*.

1972 *L'Héritage [The Inheritance]* broadcast on local Radio-Alsace and then again on France Culture (produced by Lucien Attoun) with Maria Casarès.

1973 *Récits Morts [Dead Stories]* directed by Koltès at the Théâtre du Quai. During the 1970s Koltès earned little or nothing from his writing and took casual jobs (e.g. selling tickets in Strasbourg cinemas).

1974 A second play broadcast, first on Radio Alsace and afterwards on France Culture: *Des Voix Sourdes [Deaf/Muffled Voices]*.

1975-6 Koltès moved to Paris and wrote his first novel *La Fuite à Cheval très loin dans la ville [The Flight on Horseback far into the Town]* (dated September 1976). The typescript circulated among friends for some years before being published by Les Editions de Minuit in 1984.

1977 Wrote a dramatic monologue *La Nuit juste avant les forêts [The Night just before the Forests]* for actor Yves Ferry (whom he had known at the Strasbourg Drama School) and directed him in a performance given on the fringe of the Avignon Theatre Festival. Invited by Bruno Boeglin to observe a series of actors' workshops based on the stories of J. D. Salinger and to write a play inspired by them, he wrote *Sallinger* [sic], directed by Boeglin and performed during the 1977/8 season at his El Dorado theatre in Lyon.

1978 Journey to West Africa, where he visited friends working on a construction site in Nigeria.

1979 Returned to West Africa, visiting Mali and Ivory Coast; six month trip to Nicaragua (just before the Sandanista revoultion) and to Guatemala, during which he wrote *Combat de nègre et de chiens [Black Battles with Dogs]*. The play was published as a 'tapuscrit' by Théâtre Ouvert – i.e. a limited number of typescripts which are made for circulation among theatre professionals so as to encourage the dissemination of new theatre writing.

1980 Radio broadcast on France Culture of *Combat de nègre et de chiens*. The text received its first commercial publication in the 'Théâtre Ouvert' series of Stock (Paris) together with *La Nuit juste avant les forêts*.

1981 Four month visit to New York. Koltès beginning to be known in theatre circles: *La Nuit juste avant les forêts* revived at the Petit Odéon with the actor Richard Fontana. Received a commission for a play by the Comédie Française. Plans made with Françoise Kourilsky for a production of *Combat de nègre et de chiens* in New York.

1982 Returned to New York for world première of *Combat de nègre et de chiens* at Theatre La Mama: the English translation, by Matthew Ward, was originally entitled *Come Dog, Come Night*. At Koltès's insistence, it was later changed to *Struggle of the Dogs and the Black* and published under this title, first in the collection of the New York Ubu Repertory Theatre (1982) and later by Methuen in *New French Plays* (1989). Koltès translated Athol Fugard's *The Blood Knot* for production at the Avignon Festival.

1983 Patrice Chéreau opened his new Théâtre des Amandiers at Nanterre (on the outskirts of Paris) with the French première of *Combat de nègre et de chiens*. The set (by Richard Peduzzi) was monumental and the cast star-studded: Michel Piccoli, Philippe Léotard, Myriam Boyer, Sidiki Bakaba; the critics were mostly enthusiastic: until his death at the end of the decade, Koltès was widely accepted as the most important new voice in French theatre.

From this point on he was able to live from his writing, though he earned more from foreign (especially German) productions than from the exploitation of his work in France. Worked briefly as 'dramaturge' with François Regnault on Chéreau's production of *Les Paravents [The Screens]* by Jean Genet; together they published *La Famille ds Orties [The Nettle Family]*.

1984 Journey to Senegal. Publication of *La Nuit juste avant les forêts* (see 1977). Four different productions of *Combat de nègre et de chiens* in German theatres (Frankfurt, Tübingen, Wuppertal and Munich).

1985 Publication of *Quai ouest* by Editions de Minuit; world première of the play given in Dutch at the Publiekstheater, Amsterdam.

1986 French première of *Quai ouest*, directed by Patrice Chéreau, with Maria Casarès in the cast, at the Théâtre des Amandiers. The critics were again impressed by the writing, but blamed Chéreau and Peduzzi for crushing the play beneath a monumental production. Koltès responded to a commission by the Avignon Festival for a play in a series with the title 'Oser aimer' ['To dare to love'] with a short play, *Tabataba*, about someone who 'dares to love' his motorcycle. Publication of *Dans la solitude des champs de coton [In the Solitude of the Cotton Fields]* by Minuit.

1987 First production of *Dans la solitude des champs de coton* by Patrice Chéreau at Nanterre. The role of the Client was taken by Laurent Malet and that of the Dealer by Isaach de Bankolé. In subsequent seasons Chéreau revived this production, taking the role of the Dealer himself; this provoked a temporary break with Koltès, who insisted that he had written the role of the Dealer for a black actor.

1988 Two major firsts for Koltès: *Le Retour au désert [Return to the Desert]* received its première in a production by Patrice Chéreau at the Théâtre du Rond-Point in the centre of Paris. Jacqueline Maillan, a popular comic actress for whom he had written it, was in the central role and Michel Piccoli played her brother. At the Théâtre des Amandiers his translation of *A Winter's Tale* was directed by Luc Bondy. In the metro, Koltès was struck by police 'wanted' posters with photos of the murderer Roberto Succo and became interested in his case, especially after he had seen television pictures of Succo's last hours on the roof-top of an Italian prison.

1989 Death of Koltès in Paris a week after his forty-first birthday (15th. April). Shortly before his death, he had completed his final play *Roberto Zucco*.

1990 World première of *Roberto Zucco*, directed by Peter Stein at the Berlin Schaubühne.

1997 Publication of *Plays I* by Methuen, comprising *Black Battles with Dogs* (trs. D. Bradby and M. Delgado); *Return to the Desert* (trs. D. Bradby); *Roberto Zucco* (trs. M. Crimp). First British performance of *Roberto Zucco* at the Royal Shakespeare Company at The Other Place, Stratford, directed by James MacDonald.

Chronology of plays – premières/publications (from a list by Serge Saada published in *Alternatives Théâtrales*, 35-36, June 1990).

Les Amertumes adapted from Gorki's novel *Childhood*, produced by the author, Strasbourg, 1970.

La Marche inspired by the Song of Songs, produced by the author, Strasbourg, 1971.

Procès Ivre inspired by Dostoievski's novel *Crime and Punishment*, produced by the author, Strasbourg, 1971.

L'Héritage, produced on Radio-France Alsace and then again on France-Culture (also Radio), 1972.

Récits Morts, produced by the author, Strasbourg, 1973.

Des Voix sourdes, produced on Radio-France, Alsace and on France-Culture, 1974.

Le Jour des meurtres dans l'histoire d'Hamlet, 1974.

Sallinger inspired by the stories of J.D. Salinger, produced by Bruno Boeglin, Lyon, 1977. Published by Minuit, 1995.

La Nuit juste avant les forêts monologue, produced by the author, Avignon Festival, 1977. Published by Stock/Théâtre Ouvert, 1980; Minuit, 1988. First English production as *Twilight Zone*, directed by Pierre Audi, Edinburgh Festival and Almeida Theatre, 1981.

Combat de nègre et de chiens published by Stock/Théâtre Ouvert, 1980; Minuit, 1989. First produced by Françoise Kourilsky, La Mamma theatre, New York, 1982 in a translation by Matthew Ward; first French production by Patrice Chéreau, Théâtre des Amandiers, Nanterre, 1983. First English production as *Struggle of the Black Man and the Dogs*, directed by Michael Batz, Gate Theatre, 1988. English publication: *Struggle of the Dogs and the Black* (trans. Matthew Ward) in *New French Plays*, Methuen, 1989. New English translation: *Black Battles with Dogs* (trans. David Bradby and Maria Delgado) in *Plays I*, Methuen, 1997.

Le Lien du sang translation of *The Blood Knot* by Athol Fugard, first produced by Yutaka Wada, Avignon Festival, 1982.

Quai ouest published by Minuit, 1985. First produced by Stephane Stroux in a Dutch translation, Amsterdam, 1985; first French production by Patrice Chéreau, Théâtre des Amandiers, 1986.

Tabataba produced by Hammou Graia, Avignon Festival, 1986. Published by Minuit with *Roberto Zucco* (see below).

Dans la solitude des champs de coton published by Minuit, 1986. First produced by Patrice Chéreau, Théâtre des Amandiers, 1987.

Le Conte d'hiver translation of *A Winter's Tale* by Shakespeare, first produced by Luc Bondy, Théâtre des Amandiers, 1988. Published by Minuit, 1988.

Le Retour au désert, first produced by Patrice Chéreau, Théâtre du Rond-Point, Paris, 1988. Published by Minuit, 1988. In

English: *Return to the Desert* (trans. David Bradby) in *Plays I*, Methuen, 1997.

Roberto Zucco, first produced by Peter Stein in a German translation by Simon Werle, Schaubühne, Berlin, 1990; first French production by Bruno Boeglin, Théâtre National Populaire, Villeurbanne, 1991. Published by Minuit, with *Tabataba*, 1990. In English: *Roberto Zucco* (trans. Martin Crimp) in *Plays I*, Methuen, 1997. First English production, directed by James MacDonald, The other Place, Stratford, November 1997.

Extracted from David Bradby's Chronology to
Bernard-Marie Koltès Plays : 1.
Published by Methuen Drama in 1997.

'After the second prayer you will see how the disc of the sun unfolds, and you will see hanging down from it the phallus, the origin of the wind, and when you move your face to the regions of the east it will move there, and if you move your face to the regions of the west it will follow you.'

Mithras Liturgy, part of the Great Parisian Magic Papyrus. (Quoted by Carl Jung in his last interview for the BBC.)

This play was completed in the autumn of 1988 and first performed in Berlin in April 1990. This translation of *Roberto Zucco* was first performed by the Royal Shakespeare Company on 20 November 1997 at The Other Place, Stratford-upon-Avon. The cast was as follows:

First prison officer	Archie Lal
Second prison officer	Adrian Schiller
Roberto Zucco	Zubin Varla
His Mother	Stella McCusker
A girl	Mairead McKinley
Her sister	Cathryn Bradshaw
Her brother	John Straiton
Her father	Jimmy Chisholm
Her mother	Maureen Purkis
A melancholy detective	Steve Swinscoe
Madam	Carol Macready
A panic-stricken prostitute	Penny Layden
An old gentleman	Alfred Burke
Fatman	Jake Nightingale
Police chief	Steve Swinscoe
Detective	Jimmy Chisholm
An elegant lady	Diana Kent
Her child	Ben Beeston/ Paul Drinkwater
An impatient pimp	Jake Nightingale
First police officer	Adrian Schiller
Second police officer	Archie Lal

Other parts played by members of the company

Director	James Macdonald
Set Designer	Jeremy Herbert
Costume Designer	Laura Hopkins
Lighting Designer	Nigel Edwards
Music	Joel Ryan
Fights	Terry King
Company Voice Work	Andrew Wade and Lyn Darnley

xvi

Production Manager	Benita Wakefield
Costume Supervisor	Jenny Alden
Stage Manager	Hilary Groves
Deputy Stage Manager	Suzi Blakey
Assistant Stage Manager	Elizabeth Frank

I L'évasion / Break-out

A prison surveillance post at roof level.
Prison roof-tops visible.
The time of night when prison officers, because of the silence and strain
of staring into the dark, occasionally succumb to hallucinations.

First Officer   You hear a noise?

Second Officer   No. Nothing.

Second Officer   No. Nothing.

First Officer   You never hear noises, do you?

Second Officer   Are you saying you heard a noise?

First Officer   I'm saying I think it's a possibility.

Second Officer   Well, did you or didn't you?

First Officer   Maybe not with my actual ears, but *potentially*
– yes I did.

Second Officer   Potentially but not with your actual *ears*?

First Officer   You see, the reason you never hear or see
anything is because you lack the potential.

Second Officer   The reason I never hear or see anything is
because there's never anything to see or hear. We don't have a
raison d'être, and it's because we don't have a *raison d'être* that we
always end up giving each other so much grief. Guns and
sirens that never go off, eyes wide open at a time when
everyone else has theirs tight shut – and no *raison de* fucking
être. And it seems pointless to be staring wide-eyed into space
or straining ears-pricked for non-existent sounds when our
ears should be tuned into our own inner worlds and our eyes
should be contemplating our own inner landscapes. D'you
believe in the inner world?

First Officer   I believe we have a *raison d'être* which is to
prevent escapes.

Second Officer   But this is a modern prison. Escape is not possible. Escape is not an inmate option. Not even for a tiny tiny one. Not even for a rat-sized one. Even if the bastard got through the bars he'd still have to get through the mesh. And even if he got through the mesh he'd still have to get through the membrane after the mesh. He'd have to be some kind of a liquid. And there's nothing liquid about the arm of a strangler or the hand that's stabbed a man. They're all too solid flesh, believe you me. What d'you think makes someone a potential killer? I mean not just potential but actually do it.

First Officer   Sheer evil.

Second Officer   Because I've been a prison officer for six years now, and whenever I look at a killer I ask myself what makes him different – what makes him different from a prison officer like myself who couldn't stab or strangle *any*one – not even *potentially*. I've thought and thought about this and even watched them in the showers after someone told me the killer instinct is located in a man's penis. I've seen over six hundred of them, and the fact is no two are the same – you've got your big ones, you've got your small ones, you've got your thin ones, you've got your tiny tiny ones, you've got your round ones, you've got your pointy ones, you've got your great fat thick ones – but what does it prove? Nothing.

First Officer   I'm telling you: it's sheer evil. Are you sure you can't see something?

Zucco *appears, walking along the ridge of the roof.*

Second Officer   No. Nothing.

First Officer   Neither can I – but I'm talking about *potentially*.

Second Officer   I can see some bastard walking on the roof. But that's a hallucination due to lack of sleep.

First Officer   What would some bastard be doing up on the roof anyway? You were right. There are times when we'd be better off concentrating on the inner world.

Second Officer   He even looks a bit like Roberto Zucco, the one they sent down this afternoon for killing his own father. Wild violent animal bastard.

First Officer   Roberto Zucco. Never heard of him.

Second Officer   Seriously. Can you see something? Or is it just me?

Zucco *continues to move unhurriedly along the roof.*

First Officer   Potentially I see something. The question is what?

Zucco *begins to vanish behind a chimney.*

Second Officer   An inmate escaping.

Zucco *has vanished.*

First Officer   Fuck it. You're right. It's a break-out.

Gunfire, searchlights, sirens.

II   Meurtre de la mère / He murders his mother

Zucco's **Mother** *in her nightdress in front of the locked door.*

Mother   My hand's on the phone, Roberto. I'm picking it up and I'm calling the police.

Zucco   Let me in.

Mother   Go away.

Zucco   Do I have to kick the door down? Well? Don't be so stupid.

Mother   Go on then. *Kick* it down. Kick it down and wake up the neighbours. You're sick in the head, Roberto. You were better off in prison because if they see you here they'll string you up. People don't kill their own fathers. Not in this neighbourhood. Even the dogs round here despise you.

Zucco *bangs on the door.*

How did you get out anyway? What kind of prison do they call that?

Zucco   No one will ever keep me in a prison for more than a few hours. No one. Let me in. You'd try the patience of a *snail*. Let me in or I'll smash the whole fucking place up.

Mother   What d'you think you're doing coming back here? I don't want to see your face ever again. Understand? You're not my son any more – you mean as much to me as a fly buzzing round shit.

Zucco *smashes the door down.*

Mother   Don't touch me, Roberto.

Zucco   I want my fatigues.

Mother   Your what?

Zucco   Fatigues. The khaki shirt and the combat trousers.

Mother   You mean that stupid soldier-suit? What d'you need a stupid soldier-suit for? You're mad, Roberto. If only we'd realised when you were a baby and put you out for the bin-men.

Zucco   Hurry up. Come on. I need it now.

Mother   I'll give you money. Money's what you need. Then you can buy all the stupid soldier-suits you want.

Zucco   I don't want money. I want my fatigues.

Mother   Over my dead body, Roberto. I'm calling the neighbours.

Zucco   I want my fatigues.

Mother   Don't shout at me, Roberto. Don't shout. You're frightening me. Don't shout or you'll wake the neighbours up. I can't give you those clothes. They're revolting. They're not clean. You can't go out dressed like that. At least let me wash them and dry them and put a nice crease in the trousers.

Zucco   I'll wash them myself then. I'll go to the launderette.

Mother   The launderette? You must be out of your tiny little mind.

Zucco   I love launderettes. Calm. Peaceful. And full of women.

Mother   I don't give a damn. You're not having them. Don't touch me, Roberto. I'm still in mourning for your father – are you going to kill me too?

Zucco   Come on Mum, don't be frightened. I've always been nice and kind to you, haven't I? Why be afraid? Why not just give me my fatigues? I need them, Mum, I really need them.

Mother   I don't want you to be nice to me, Roberto. Do you really expect me to forget that you killed your own father? That you tossed him out of the window the way other people toss a cigarette? And then you start being nice to me? I don't want to forget you killed your father, Roberto – and if you're nice to me, I'll forget everything.

Zucco   That's right, Mum. Forget. Give me my fatigues. The khaki shirt and the combat trousers. Clean or not. Pressed or not. Give them to me. And then I promise you I'll go.

Mother   I can't believe I gave birth to you, Roberto. I can't believe you were ever inside of me. If it hadn't been in this room, if I hadn't seen you come out of my own body and watched you being laid in the cradle – if I hadn't seen you since the cradle grow and change, watching you so closely that I didn't even notice the changes happening – and if you suddenly now appeared in front of me and said you were the son I gave birth to in this bed, I'd refuse to believe you. But I recognise you, Roberto. I recognise you only too well – the size and the shape of your body – the colour of your hair and of your eyes – the shape of your hands – those huge strong hands of yours which you've only ever used to stroke your mother's neck – and grab hold of your father's – the father you killed. What makes a boy who's been so good for twenty-four years suddenly go insane? What makes him leave the rails, Roberto? Who put the tree across the straight and narrow track and forced you over the edge? Roberto, Roberto, when a car is wrecked at the bottom of the ravine you don't repair it. When a train goes off the rails you don't try and put it back on the tracks. You leave it. You forget it. And I'll forget you, Roberto. You're already forgotten.

Zucco   Before you forget me completely, you can tell me where my fatigues are.

Mother   Over there. Screwed up in the basket. I told you: they're filthy. (**Zucco** *gets them out.*) Now get out like you promised.

Zucco   Yes. Like I promised.

He goes up to her, strokes her, kisses her, grips her. She moans.

When he lets go she drops to the floor, strangled.

Zucco *undresses, slips on the fatigues and goes.*

III   Sous la table / Under the table

In the kitchen.
A table covered with a cloth reaching to the ground.
The **Girl***'s* **Sister** *appears.*
She goes to the window and opens it part way.

Sister   Inside. Quietly. Shoes off. Sit down and shut up.

The **Girl** *climbs in through the window.*

Sister: And so, in the middle of the night, I finally discover you squatting against a wall. Your brother's taken the car – he's searching the whole city – he's out of his mind with worry – and believe you me he'll have more than your pants down when he finds you. Your mother's been glued to the window for hours imagining everything imaginable from gang-rape by a bunch of thugs to finding your dismembered body in the woods – not to mention being trapped in the cellar by a psychopath – you name it. Your father's so convinced he'll

never see you again he's got himself totally pissed and now
he's snoring on the sofa – snoring his sick heart out. And here
am I, here am I running round the neighbourhood like an
idiot while all the time you're squatting there against a wall.
Why couldn't you just've crossed the yard and set our minds
at rest? What did you hope to achieve? Because believe
you me he'll have your pants down. And I hope he makes
you bleed.

Pause.

So, I see you've decided not to talk to me. You've decided
silence is more dramatic. Silence. Silence. Silence. Panic all
around but I'm not telling. My lips are sealed. Well we'll see
just how sealed they really are when your brother gets your
pants down. Open that little mouth of yours and explain to me
why you were back so late when you were told midnight.
Because if you don't open that little mouth I'm going to start
panicking, I'm going to start imagining all kinds of things, just
like the others. Come on, my baby robin. Tell your sister.
Whatever it is, I'll understand. And if he's violent, I promise
I'll protect you.

Pause.

It's a boy, isn't it. You've been out with some boy. Some
typical idiot boy. What did he do? Fumble about? Grope you
about? We've all been there, my little lovebird. We've all been
babies. We've all been to parties with those idiot boys. Getting
kissed can't hurt you. You'll get kissed by plenty of idiot boys
whether you like it or not. You'll get their idiot hands up your
skirt whether you want it or not. Because boys have no brains
and putting their hands up a girl's skirt is the best they can
manage. They absolutely love it. I don't know what they get
out of it. Nothing at all if you ask me. It's just what they do.
They can't help themselves. They were born like that –
mentally defective. But it's not worth making a scene about.
What matters is that they don't take from you that thing, that
thing which must not be taken from you before the time
comes. But I know that you will wait until the time comes, the
time when all of us – your mother, your father, your brother,

myself, and you too, obviously – will choose who to give it to.
Unless someone's used force. And who'd dare to use force on
such a pure innocent child? Well? Tell me no one has used
force. Tell me, please tell me no one has taken the thing which
must not be taken. Talk to me. Talk to me or I'm going to get
very angry. (*A noise.*) Quickly. Under the table. It sounds like
your brother.

*The **Girl** disappears under the table.*

*Their **Father** enters, half asleep, in his pyjamas. He goes through the
kitchen, vanishes for a moment, reappears and goes back to his room.*

Sister   You're still a child. You're still a virgin. You still
belong to your sister, to your brother, to your father and to
your mother. I don't want to hear this. It's horrible. Shut up.
I'm going mad. You've thrown yourself away, and dragged
the rest of us with you.

*Their **Brother** comes crashing in. The **Sister** throws herself at him.*

Calm down and don't start shouting. She's not here but she
has been found. She has been found but she isn't here. Calm
down or I'll go mad. Don't make things worse by shouting or
I'll kill myself.

Brother   Where is she? *Tell* me.

Sister   At a friend's. Sleeping at a friend's. Warm and safe
in her friend's bed. Nothing – believe me – can hurt her.
Something truly terrible has happened. Don't start shouting.
Please. Don't. You know you'll regret it. You know you'll end
up in tears.

Brother   I'll only end up in tears if something truly terrible
has happened to my baby sister. I've kept such a close eye on
her and this is the only night she's got away – the only night
she's got away from me in all these years and years of
watching. It takes more time than that for evil to destroy
someone.

Sister   Evil doesn't take time. It comes when it wants and in
a moment it changes everything. In one moment it can smash

the precious object you've spent – yes – years protecting.

She takes an object and drops it on the floor.

And you can't put back the pieces. You can scream and you can shout, but you can't put back the pieces.

Their **Father** *enters. He crosses the room as before and disappears.*

Brother   Help me. Please. Help me. You're stronger than me. I can't deal with evil.

Sister   No one can deal with evil.

Brother   But you can help me.

Sister   Not deal with evil, no.

Brother   Christ, I need a drink. (*He goes out.*)

Their **Father** *reappears.*

Father   What's this then? Crying? Did I hear someone crying?

(**Sister** *gets up.*)

Sister   I was singing to myself, that's all. (*She goes out.*)

Father   So you should. It wards off evil. (*He goes out.*)

A moment passes, then the **Girl** *emerges from under the table, goes to the window and lets in* **Zucco**.

Girl   Take your shoes off. What's your name?

Zucco   Whatever you like. What's yours?

Girl   I don't have a name any more. Little this, little that – little robin, little lovebird, little cuckoo, little sparrow, little nightingale or skylark, little dove – that's all they ever call me. I'd prefer little pig, little rattlesnake or little rat. What do you do in real life?

Zucco   In real life?

Girl   Real life, yes – your work, your job, how you earn money – the things people do.

Zucco   I don't do the things people do.

Girl   Then what *do* you do?

Zucco   I'm a secret agent. D'you know what a secret agent is?

Girl   I know what a secret is.

Zucco   Secret agents aren't just secret. They travel. They go all over the world. And have guns.

Girl   Have you got a gun?

Zucco   Of course I've got a gun.

Girl   Show me then.

Zucco   No.

Girl   Then you haven't got a gun.

Zucco   I've got this. (*Takes out knife.*)

Girl   That's not a gun.

Zucco   It's just as good for killing people.

Girl   What else do secret agents do, apart from kill people?

Zucco   Travel. Go to Africa. D'you know Africa?

Girl   Of course.

Zucco   I know places in Africa where the mountains are so high it always snows. No one knows it snows in Africa. But it's the best thing in the world: African snow falling on the frozen African lakes.

Girl   I'd love to see African snow. I'd love to skate on the frozen lakes.

Zucco   And walking across the snow-covered lakes there are white rhinoceroses.

Girl   What's your name? Tell me your name.

Zucco   I won't ever tell my name.

Girl Why not? I want to know your name.

Zucco It's a secret.

Girl I can keep secrets. Tell me your name.

Zucco Can't remember.

Girl Liar.

Zucco Andreas.

Girl No.

Zucco Angelo.

Girl I'm going to scream if you make fun of me. It's not any of those stupid names.

Zucco How d'you know that when you don't know what it is?

Girl It can't be. I'd recognise it straight away.

Zucco I can't tell you.

Girl Even if you can't tell me, tell me anyway.

Zucco I can't. Something terrible could happen.

Girl So what? Tell me anyway.

Zucco If I told you, I'd die.

Girl Even if you have to die, tell me anyway.

Zucco Roberto.

Girl Roberto what?

Zucco Come on. That's enough.

Girl Roberto what? If you don't tell me I'll scream, and my brother who's very very angry will come and kill you.

Zucco When you told me you knew what a secret was, did you really mean it?

Girl It's the only thing I really do really know. Tell me your name, tell me your name.

Zucco   Roberto Zucco.

Girl   I'll never forget that name. Hide under the table. Someone's coming.

Her **Mother** *enters.*

Mother   Talking to yourself, my little nightingale?

Girl   Just singing to ward off evil.

Mother   So you should. (*Sees the broken object.*) Thank God. I never could stand the sight of that piece of shit.

Mother *goes out.*

The **Girl** *joins* **Zucco** *under the table.*

Girl's voice   Listen to me: you've taken my virginity, and it's yours to keep. No one else can take it from me now. You'll have it for the rest of your life, even when you've forgotten me, even when you're dead. I've marked you for life like a scar after a fight. And I'm not likely to forget, because I don't have another one to give away to anyone. It's finished. It's gone. Till the day I die. I've given it away and now it's yours.

IV   La mélancolie de l'inspecteur / The melancholy detective

Brothel reception in Little Chicago.

Detective   I'm not a happy man. I'm sick at heart and I just can't fathom it. I'm often unhappy but this time something jars. Usually when I feel like this and get the urge to weep – or die – I try and find an explanation. I go back over everything that's happened during the day, the night, the previous day – and I always end up discovering some insignificant event which – however meaningless at the time – has stuck in me like some bastard of a bug tearing my guts apart. And once I've identified the meaningless event giving me so much grief then I'm laughing. Bug eliminated – like a louse by a fingernail – end of story. But this time it's different. I've traced and retraced every step of the past three days only to end up back where I started: none the wiser, none the happier, and sick to the heart.

Madam   Too much tinkering with pimps and dead bodies, Inspector.

Detective   There are less dead bodies than people think. But yes – you're right – far too many pimps. My policy would be minimise pimps, maximise dead bodies.

Madam   Give me a pimp any day – I'd rather make my living out of the living.

Detective   Well I must be on my way. Goodbye.

Zucco *emerges from a room and locks the door.*

Madam   Never say goodbye, Inspector.

The **Detective** *leaves, followed by* **Zucco***.*

After a few moments a panic-stricken **Prostitute** *comes in.*

Prostitute   *Madame, Madame,* the forces of darkness have just swept through the streets of Little Chicago. The neighbourhood's stunned. The girls can't work. The pimps can't speak. The clients have fled. Everything's stopped. Everything's paralysed. *Madame,* you've harboured a devil in this house. That boy who just came, who never opened his lips, who never answered the girls' questions, who seemed speechless, sexless, but had such a gentle face – rather good-looking actually and gave us girls a lot to talk about – you should've seen the way he followed the Inspector out. We're all watching him, having a laugh, making various suppositions. He's walking right behind the Inspector who seems absorbed by some profound problem – walking right behind him like his own shadow, like a shadow shrinking in the midday sun, getting closer and closer to the hunched body of the Inspector – when suddenly he pulls a long knife out of his jacket pocket and buries it in the poor man's back. The Inspector stops. Doesn't turn round. Gently nods his head as if the profound problem he was absorbed in has finally been solved. Then his whole body sways, and he collapses on the ground. Not for one moment have the eyes of the murderer met the eyes of the victim. The boy had been staring at the Inspector's revolver – and now he bends down, removes it, pockets it, and calmly continues on his way, as calmly as the Antichrist, *Madame*. Because nobody moved. Everyone just stood there watching him go. Watching him vanish into the crowd. It was the devil himself, *Madame*. And he was in this house.

Madam   Devil or not, kill an Inspector and the boy's as good as fucked.

V   Le Frangin / Brotherly Love

Kitchen.
Girl *against the wall, in a state of terror.*

Brother   Don't be scared of me, chicken. I'm not going to hurt you. Your sister's an idiot. What made her think I was going to hit you? You're cunt now – I never hit cunt. I like cunt – cunt's what I prefer. I certainly prefer it to a baby sister. A baby sister's a pain in the neck. You have to keep your eye on her all the time, keep on the alert. And to protect her what? Her *virginity*? Because just how long are you supposed to keep your eye on your sister's virginity? All that time I've spent watching over you is now totally wasted. And I regret every moment. I regret every wasted day and every wasted hour. Girls should be fucked and off their big brothers' backs as soon as it's physically possible – then there'd be nothing left to protect and we could spend our time on better things. So I'm not complaining if you've gone and got yourself laid – in fact it's a weight off my mind. It means we can go our separate ways without dragging you behind me like a ball and chain. Tell you what: let's go and have a drink. It's time you learned to stop blushing and staring at the floor. Forget all that. It's over. Shock the bastards. Get your head up, look them in the eye, stare them out, they love that. There's no point holding yourself back another second, sweetheart. Just go for it. Fuck

it. Do it. Hang out in Little Chicago with the working girls.
Get on the game. You'll earn yourself some cash and be
responsible to no one. And perhaps I'll meet you working the
bars, and nod ever so slightly – out of brotherly love – and
we'll have a fucking good brotherly sisterly time, eh? So don't
waste your energy staring at the floor with your legs squeezed
together, chicken, because what is the point? I mean you can
forget marriage. Yes it made sense saving you for a husband.
Yes it made sense staring at the floor waiting for your
wedding-day. But wedding-days are now fucked – and
everything else is now fucked. Marriage, family, father,
mother, sister – all totally fucked in one fell swoop and I don't
give a shit. Your father snoring his heart out. Your mother in
tears. Far better leave them to their snores and tears and quit
this house. Get pregnant if you like – who cares? Or not. Who
gives a shit? Do just what you like. I'm not your guardian any
more. You're not a little girl any more. You don't have an age
now – fifteen or fifty, it's all the same. What you are is cunt.
And no one gives a toss.

VI   Métro / Metro

A wanted poster with an un-named picture of **Zucco**.
Caption: 'Have you seen this man?'
Beneath it, side by side on a bench, an **Old Gentleman** *and*
Zucco.
The station has shut down for the night.

Old Gentleman   I'm an old man and it's not sensible for
me to be out this late. I was still congratulating myself for
having caught the last train when – come to a fork in this
labyrinth of corridors and stairways – I suddenly realised I'd
lost my bearings – even though I use this station so often that I
thought I knew it like I know my own kitchen. I had no idea
that beyond my tried and trusted everyday track there lurked
a dark world of tunnels and unknown paths of which I would
rather quite frankly have remained in ignorance, if my stupid
absentmindedness hadn't forced me to make their

acquaintance. Just like that the lights went out, leaving only these little white lamps of whose existence I was utterly unaware, and myself walking on and on as fast as I could through an unfamiliar world – not that 'fast' means much for an old man like me. And just when at the end of endless motionless escalators I thought I could see a way out – crash! – down comes a vast metal shutter. So here I am, in a rather peculiar situation for a man of my age, a victim of absentmindedness and a lack of agility, not quite sure what I'm waiting for, and not quite sure quite frankly that I want to be sure, since at my time of life new experiences are hard to swallow. Dawn, I suppose. Yes, I suppose I'm waiting for the dawn here in this station which seemed as familiar to me as my own kitchen before it became so frightening. I suppose I'm waiting for the lights to come back on and for the first train to pass by. But what worries me is how the daylight will look after this ludicrous adventure. And this station will never be the same. I'll always be aware of these little white lamps which previously did not exist. And staying up through the night – I've never done it before – who knows how one's life could be altered? – everything must get out of step – nights won't follow days the way they used to. I find that all very disturbing. But as for you, young man, who seem as clear-headed as you are able-bodied – yes – whose clear gaze is so obviously not the dull and foolish gaze of an old man such as myself, it's impossible to believe that you have let yourself be ensnared by all these corridors and steel shutters – since steel shutters or not, surely a young clear-headed boy like you could slip right through them like a drop of water through a sieve. Do you work nights here? Tell me about yourself and set my mind at rest.

Zucco   I'm just a normal sensible young man who never draws attention to himself. Would you have even noticed me if I wasn't sitting right next to you? I've always thought that the best way to live in peace is to be as transparent as a pane of glass, like a chameleon on a stone – to walk through walls – to have no colour or smell – so people see right through you to the people on the other side, as if you just weren't there. It's

no easy job to be transparent. It takes dedication. To be
invisible is an old – an ancient dream. I'm not a hero. Heroes
are criminals. There's not one hero whose clothes aren't
steeped in blood – and blood is the one thing in the world that
never goes unnoticed. The thing most visible in all the world.
When the end finally comes, and the earth is smothered by the
smoke of destruction, the blood-drenched rags of heroes will
remain. You're talking to a student – a good one. Learn to be
a good student and you never look back. I have a place at
university – on the ancient benches of the Sorbonne – a seat
reserved in the middle of all those other good students who
don't even notice me. Because believe you me you need to be
a good student – invisible and discreet – to go to the
Sorbonne. It's not one of these red-brick places full of yobs
and people who think they're heroes. In my university
shadowy figures pace the silent corridors and their footsteps
make no sound. Starting tomorrow I'm going back to my
linguistics course. Tomorrow, you see, is linguistics day. And
there I'll be – an invisible man among invisible men – silent
and attentive behind the smokescreen of everyday life.
Nothing can change the course of things, nothing. I calmly
cross the prairie like a train that can never leave the tracks.
I'm like a hippopotamus moving very slowly through the mud,
whose chosen path and pace nothing can alter.

Old Gentleman   You can always leave the tracks, young
man. Anyone – as I now know – can leave the tracks at any
moment. Even an old man, even a man like myself who
thought he knew life and the world like his own kitchen can be
suddenly – crash! – shut out of the world – at this nothing
o'clock – in this unnatural light – full of fear of what may
happen when the lights come back on and the trains begin
and the station fills with people as ordinary as I once used to
be – and after my first night without sleep I'll have no choice
but to go out past the now open shutters and, without having
witnessed the night, confront the day. And now I've no idea
what will happen. How will I see the world? And how will the
world see – or fail to see – me? I won't know which is day and
which is night – I won't know what to do – I'll be pacing up

and down in my kitchen searching for the right time and quite frankly, young man, it's all making me rather afraid.

Zucco   Well you have every reason to be.

Old Gentleman   You have a very slight stammer, which I find rather attractive. It puts me at my ease. When the chaos here begins, would you help me? Would you help a lost old man like myself to the exit? If not beyond?

The lights come back on.

Zucco *helps the* **Old Gentleman** *get up, and leads him away as the first train passes.*

VII   Deux sœurs / Two sisters

The kitchen.
The **Girl** *with a bag.*
Her **Sister** *appears.*

Sister   I forbid you to leave.

Girl   You won't forbid me anything. From now on I'm the grown-up.

Sister   A grown-up? You? You're a baby robin perched on a branch. And I'm your big sister.

Girl   Big virgin more like it. You don't know anything about life – you've always looked out for yourself – you've always looked after yourself. I'm the grown-up, *I* was raped, I'm the one with nothing left to lose, and I'll make my own decisions.

Sister   But you're my baby sister who told me all her little secrets!

Girl   And you're an old maid who knows nothing about anything, has no experience and ought to keep her mouth shut!

Sister   What d'you mean, experience? Bad experiences are no use to anyone. All you can do is try and forget them as

quickly as possible. Only the good experiences worth having.
You'll always remember the beautiful quiet evenings you spent
with your parents, your brother and your sister – they'll stay
with you even when you're old. Whereas you'll soon forget
this tragedy of ours, my little cuckoo, under your sister, your
brother and your parents' watchful eye.

Girl   It's my parents, my brother and my sister I want to
forget – not my so-called tragedy.

Sister   Your brother will take good care of you, my little
skylark. How could anyone love you as much as he does – a
man who's always loved you more than he's loved anyone?
One man who's all the men you'll ever need.

Girl   I don't want to be loved.

Sister   How can you say that? It's the only thing in this life
that matters.

Girl   How dare you? You've never even had a man. You've
never even *been* loved. You've spent your whole life totally
unhappy and totally alone.

Sister   I've never been unhappy except on account of your
unhappiness.

Girl   Oh yes you have been very unhappy: all those times
I've caught you crying behind the curtains.

Sister   I cry at set times for no reason – just to build up
credit – and now I've built up all that credit, you'll never see
me cry again. Why d'you want to leave?

Girl   To find him again.

Sister   You'll never find him again.

Girl   I know I'll find him again.

Sister   Rubbish. You know perfectly well your brother's
been trying to for days and nights on end. To avenge you.

Girl   But I don't want to be 'avenged'. That's why I'll find
him.

Sister   And what will you do when you do find him?

Girl   Tell him something.

Sister   What?

Girl   Something.

Sister   And where d'you think he is?

Girl   Little Chicago.

Sister   Why does my innocent dove want to throw herself away? Please, don't leave me. Don't leave me alone here. Not with your brother and your parents. Not alone in this house. Without you, my life will be worth nothing, nothing will make sense any more. Don't leave me. I'm begging you not to leave me. I hate your brother and your parents and this house. You're all I've got to love, my innocent innocent dove, and all I've got to live for.

Their **Father** *enters in a rage.*

Father   Your mother's hidden the beer. I'll knock her fucking senseless like the good old days. Why did I ever stop? True it wore me out, but I should've made myself, drilled myself, or had the job done professionally. I should've kept it up like the good old days – set times – regular beatings. But now look – turn a blind eye and the next thing you know she's hidden the beer you conniving little bitches. (*He looks under the table*) I had five bottles left and if they don't turn up I'll hit you five times each.

He goes.

Sister   My turtledove in Little Chicago! You must be – and you will be – so unhappy!

Their **Mother** *enters.*

Mother   Your father's drunk again. The cretin knocks back the beer, bottle after bottle, and what do the pair of you do? Just stand there. Just stand there and leave it up to me to fight the drunken bastard. Just stand there and watch him ruin us with his drinking. You're a pair of little idiots with your chatter chatter chatter. All you care about is your own stupid little problems while I'm left to deal with that piss-artist. What're you doing with that bag?

Sister   She's going to spend the night at a friend's.

Mother   At a friend's, at a friend's? What friend? What are you girls up to? Why does she need to spend the night at a friend's? Aren't the beds here good enough? Aren't the nights here dark enough? If you were younger and I was stronger I'd crack your heads together.

She goes.

Sister   I don't want you to be unhappy.

Girl   But I'm happy to be unhappy. Yes, there was a lot of pain, but the pain's what I enjoyed.

Sister   I'll die if you leave me.

The **Girl** *picks up the bag and goes.*

VIII   Juste avant de mourir / Just before dying

Outside a late-night bar. Phone-booth.
With a great crash of broken glass, **Zucco** *comes flying through the window.*
Screams from within. A crowd of onlookers appears at the doorway.

Zucco   'And thus was I created like the statue
    Of an athlete standing on a holy
    Pedestal, perfected by the fury
    Of the tempestuous sea raging vainly
        At my feet. Strong and naked, my brow thrust . . .'

Prostitute   He'll catch his death. It's fucking freezing out here.

Bloke   Don't you worry about him. He's sweating. He's plenty warm enough inside.

Zucco   '. . . Into the abyss; hail and foam-enveloped;
Buffeted by the storm-wracked nights, I raise
These arms towards th' ethereal darkness.'

Bloke   Pissed out of his head.

Bloke   Rubbish. He's not been drinking.

Prostitute   He's just crazy. Why can't you leave him alone?

Fatman   Leave him alone? He pisses us all about for hours
on end and you say leave him alone? One more time and I'll
crack his skull open.

Prostitute *(goes to help* **Zucco** *up)*   No more fighting. Come
on. No more fighting. You've already messed up that beautiful
face of yours. Don't you want the girls to look at you any
more? Faces are precious, lover-boy. You think a face is for
life, then it's rearranged by some ugly bastard with no face to
lose. But you've got so *much* to lose, lover-boy. Your face is like
your balls – lose it and your whole life's fucked. You don't
care now, but believe me, you will do in the morning. Don't
look at me like that or I'll start to cry – you're the sort who can
make people cry just by looking at them.

Zucco *goes up to* **Fatman** *and punches him.*

Prostitute   They're not going to start again?

Fatman   Don't tempt me, my friend, just don't tempt me.

Zucco *punches him again.* **Fatman** *hits back. They fight.*

Prostitute   I'm calling the police. He's going to kill him.

Bloke   You're not calling anyone.

Bloke   And anyway, he's out for the count.

Zucco *gets up and follows* **Fatman** *as he moves away. He clings on
to him and punches him in the face.*

Prostitute   Ignore him. Leave him alone. He can hardly
stand up.

Zucco   Come on. Fight. You gutless bollockless bastard.

Fatman *sends him flying.*

Fatman   He tries that again and I squash him like a fly.

Again **Zucco** *gets up and tries to make him fight.*

Prostitute (*to* **Fatman**)   Don't hurt him, don't hurt him, you'll cripple him.

Fatman *knocks* **Zucco** *out.*

Bloke   That's flattened the bastard.

Prostitute   It wasn't a fair fight. He's right you've got no guts.

Fatman   A man doesn't let the same dog bite twice.

They go back into the bar.

Zucco *gets up and goes to the phone-booth.*

He picks up the phone, dials, and waits.

Zucco   Take me away. Take me away from here. It's too hot in this fuck of a city. Take me to snowy Africa. Take me there before I die. Because nobody cares about anyone. Not anyone. The men need women and the women need men – but as for love, there *is* none. I get a hard-on with women out of sheer pity. I'd like to come back as a dog, to find a little happiness. A stray dog no one would notice, poking round the bins. I'd like to be the kind of yellow scab-infested stray people automatically avoid, poking round the bins till the end of time. What use are words when there's nothing to be said? They should stop teaching words. They should close the schools and enlarge the cemeteries. Anyway – one year or a hundred – what difference does it make? Sooner or later we all of us have to die. And that's what makes the birds sing, and that's what makes them laugh at us.

Prostitute (*in the doorway*)   I told you he was mad. That phone doesn't even work.

Zucco *drops the phone and sits back against the booth.*

Fatman *comes over.*

Fatman   What's on your mind, my friend?

Zucco   I'm dreaming about the immortality of the crab, the slug, and the dung-beetle.

Fatman   Listen, my friend, I don't enjoy fighting. But there are limits to what a man can take, limits to how far he can be pushed. Why push me so far, eh? You want to die, or what?

Zucco   I don't *want* to die. I'm *going* to die.

Fatman   Like everyone else, my friend.

Zucco   That's not a reason.

Fatman   Maybe not.

Zucco   The trouble with beer is you think you're buying it but you're only renting it. I need a piss.

Fatman   Go on then – before it's too late.

Zucco   Is it true that even the dogs despise me?

Fatman   Dogs don't despise anyone. Dogs are the only creatures you can trust. They love you or they hate you, but they never judge you. And when everyone's washed their hands of you, my friend, there'll still be some dog somewhere waiting to lick the soles of your feet.

Zucco   'Morte villana, di pietà nemica,
   di dolor madre antica,
   giudicio incontastabile gravoso,
   di te blasmar la lingua s'affatica.'

Fatman   What about that piss?

Zucco   Too late.

Dawn breaks.

Zucco *falls asleep.*

IX   Dalila / Delilah

A Police Station. A **Detective** *and a* **Chief Of Police**.
The **Girl** *enters, followed by her* **Brother**, *who stays close to the door.*
The **Girl** *goes up to* **Zucco***'s picture and points to it.*

Girl   I know him.

Chief   Know him? Really?

Girl   Yes. Really. Extremely well.

Detective   Who is he then?

Girl   A secret agent. A friend.

Detective   What about that character over there?

Girl   My brother. He's come with me. I recognised that
photo in the street and he said to come.

Detective   You realise he's wanted by the police?

Girl   Yes. And I want him too.

Detective   And you're saying this is a friend of yours?

Girl   A friend, yes, a friend.

Detective   The killer – of a policeman. You'll be arrested
and charged with conspiracy, concealment of weapons, and
failure to report a criminal.

Girl   But my brother said to come and say I know him. I'm
not concealing anything, I'm not reporting anyone. I know
him, that's all.

Detective   Tell your brother he can go.

Chief   Are you deaf? Get out.

The **Brother** *leaves.*

Detective   What can you tell us about him?

Girl   Everything.

Detective   French? Foreign?

Girl   He had a really faint but really really nice – yes – accent.

Chief   Germanic?

Girl   I don't know what 'Germanic' means.

Detective   So. . . he *told* you he was a secret agent. That's strange. Secret agents don't as a rule reveal the fact.

Girl   I told him I'd keep it a secret whatever happened.

Chief   Congratulations. If everyone kept secrets like that our job would be simple.

Girl   He told me he went on missions to Africa – in the mountains – where it snows all the time.

Detective   A German agent in Kenya.

Chief   So Police theories weren't so off the mark after all.

Detective   Accurate in the extreme, Chief. (*To* **Girl**) What about his name? D'you know it? You must if he's your friend.

Girl   Yes, I know it.

Chief   Tell us.

Girl   I know it really well.

Chief   Don't make fun of the police, young lady – unless you'd like a few bruises to take home.

Girl   I don't want any bruises. I know his name, but I just can't say it.

Detective   What d'you mean: you just can't say it?

Girl   It's right on the tip of my tongue.

Chief   Tip of your tongue, tip of your tongue? How'd you like to be slapped and punched and have your hair pulled out, eh? We have rooms here purpose-built. Understand?

Girl   No. Please. It's there. It will come.

Detective   How about his first name? You must remember

that. You must've slobbered it in his ear often enough.

Chief   Come on – first name – any name – or it's off to the torture chamber.

Girl   Andreas.

Detective (*to* **Chief**)   Andreas. Now we're talking. (*to* **Girl**) Are you sure?

Girl   No.

Chief   I'm going to kill her.

Detective   Out with the bastard's name or you get a knuckle-fucking-sandwich. Hurry up. I'm warning you.

Girl   Angelo.

Detective   Spanish.

Chief   Or Italian, or Brazilian, or Portuguese, or Mexican. I've even come across a Berliner called Julio.

Detective   You're a true man of the world, chief. (*to* **Girl**) I'm losing my patience.

Girl   I can feel it on my lips.

Chief   Fancy a smack on the lips to help it on its way?

Girl   Angelo. Angelo. Che. Dolce. Or something like that.

Detective   Dolce? As in sweet?

Girl   Yes, as in sweet. He told me his name was like a foreign word for sweet or sugary. (*She begins to cry*) He was so sweet and kind.

Detective   I suppose there must be lots of foreign words for sweet or sugary.

Chief   Azucarado, zuccherato, glykos, gezuckert, ocukrzony.

Detective   To name but five, chief.

Girl   Zucco. Zucco. Roberto Zucco.

Detective   Are you positive?

Girl   Yes. Positive.

Chief   Zucco. With a Z?

Girl   With a Z, yes. Roberto with a Z.

Detective   Take her to make a statement.

Girl   What about my brother?

Chief   Brother? What brother? Who needs a brother when you've got us?

They all go out.

X   L'otage / The Hostage

A park in broad daylight.
An elegant lady sitting on a bench.
Enter **Zucco**.

Lady   Sit here beside me. Talk to me. I'm bored – let's have a conversation. I hate parks. Don't be shy. Do I intimidate you?

Zucco   I'm not shy.

Lady   But your hands are shaking like a boy about to have his first taste of sex. You have a nice face. You're a good-looking boy. Do you like women? You're almost too good-looking to like women.

Zucco   I like women. I like them a lot.

Lady   I suppose you mean these ridiculous eighteen-year-olds.

Zucco   I like all women.

Lady   Well that's excellent. And have you been brutal yet with a woman?

Zucco   Never.

Lady   Not even felt the desire? Surely you've at least felt the desire to treat one violently? It's a desire all men have had at some point. Without exception.

Zucco   Not me. I'm gentle and peace-loving.

Lady   You're a strange sort of person.

Zucco   Did you come in a taxi?

Lady   Certainly not. I can't bear taxi-drivers.

Zucco   So you came in a car.

Lady   Obviously. I didn't walk here – I live on the other side of town.

Zucco   What make's the car?

Lady   What – did you think it was a Porsche? No, it's a pathetic little car. My husband's a tight bastard.

Zucco   What make?

Lady   Mercedes.

Zucco   Which model?

Lady   280 SE.

Zucco   That's not a pathetic little car.

Lady   Maybe not – but he's a tight bastard all the same.

Zucco   What's that guy playing at? Why does he keep looking at you?

Lady   That's my son.

Zucco   Your son? But he's big.

Lady   Not a day over fourteen. I'm not geriatric, you know.

Zucco   He looks older than that. Does he do sport?

Lady   That's all he *ever* does. Not only am I paying for him to belong to every club in town – tennis, hockey, golf – but then he expects me to ferry him about to training sessions. He's a little prick, actually.

Zucco   He looks strong for his age. Give me your car-keys.

Lady   Of course. My pleasure. I suppose you want the car as well.

Zucco   Yes. The car as well.

Lady   Take it.

Zucco   Give me the keys.

Lady   Oh don't be so boring.

Zucco   Give me the keys.

He gets out the gun and puts it on his lap.

Lady   You must be mad. You don't play with a thing like that.

Zucco   Call your son.

Lady   Certainly not.

Zucco (*threatens her with the gun*)   Call your son.

Lady   You must be out of your mind. (*Shouts to her son.*) Run for it. Go back home. Just get the hell out.

As her son approaches, the **Lady** *gets up.* **Zucco** *holds the gun to her throat.*

Lady   Shoot me then, you idiot. I won't give you the keys – if only so you don't take me for a fool. My husband takes me for a fool, my son takes me for a fool, the maid takes me for a fool, so go on – shoot – it'll be one less fool. But you're not getting the keys. And oh dear, what a shame – because it's a superb car – leather seats, and dashboard in figured walnut. Oh dear, what a shame. Just stop making a scene. Look – those idiots are going to come over and start making comments. They'll call the police. Just look at the way they're licking their lips. It's their lucky day. I can't bear those people and their bloody comments. Go on: shoot. I don't want to hear them. I don't want to hear.

Zucco (*to the* **Child**)   Keep back.

Man   Look at the way he's shaking.

Zucco   For christsake keep back. On the ground. Lie down.

Woman   It's the child making him afraid.

Zucco   Now – hands by your sides. Come closer. Crawl.

Woman   How's he supposed to crawl with his hands by his sides?

Man: It's not impossible. *I* could do it.

Zucco   Slowly. Hands behind your back. Keep your head down. Stop. (*The* **Child** *makes a movement.*) Don't move a muscle or I'm killing your mother.

Man   He's not joking either.

Woman   Absolutely. He's going to do it. Poor kid.

Zucco   Promise you won't move?

Child   Promise.

Zucco   Keep your head right down on the ground. Turn round slowly so you're facing the other way. Turn round. I don't want you to be able to see us.

Child   But why are you afraid of me? What can *I* do? I'm a child. I don't want my mother killed. There's no reason for you to be afraid of me – you're much stronger than I am.

Zucco   Much stronger. Yes.

Child   So why are you afraid of me? What could I do to you? I'm too small.

Zucco   Not so small as all that – and I'm not afraid.

Child   Yes you are. You're shaking. You're shaking. I can hear it in your voice.

Man   Here come the police.

Woman   Now he'll have something to shake about.

Man   This should be a laugh.

Zucco (*to* **Child**)   Shut your eyes.

Child   They *are* shut, they *are* shut. *Christ* you're a coward.

Zucco   Shut your mouth too.

Child   I'll shut whatever you like – but you're still a coward – frightening a woman – pointing that stupid gun at a woman.

Zucco   Your mother's car – what kind is it?

Child   Might be a Porsche.

Zucco   Shut up. Shut your face. Shut your mouth. Shut your eyes. Play dead.

Child   I don't know how to play dead.

Zucco   You'll soon find out. I'll kill your mother – then you'll see what playing dead means.

Woman   Poor kid.

Child   I'm playing dead, I'm playing dead.

Man   The police are keeping their distance.

Woman   Shit-scared, that's why.

Man   Not at all. It's strategy. They know what they're doing. We may not understand their tactics – but they know what they're doing, believe you me. He's basically had it.

Man   The woman too, if you ask me.

Man   Well you can't make an omelette without breaking the eggs.

Woman   Just don't let him hurt the kid– please God, not the kid.

Forcing the **Lady** *forwards with the gun to her neck,* **Zucco** *goes up to the* **Child** *and puts one foot on his head.*

Woman   Dear me, children these days have a pretty rough time of it.

Man   Well we had a pretty rough time of it when *we* were kids.

Woman   And I suppose *you* were threatened by a psychopath, were you?

Man   I'm talking about the war actually – or have you forgotten?

Woman   Oh really? I suppose the Germans trod on *your* face and attacked *your* mother, did they?

Man   Worse than that actually, if you really want to know.

Woman   Well it didn't stop you getting old and fat and living to tell the tale, did it.

Man   There's no need to be offensive.

Woman   My only concern is for the child – just for the child.

Man   For godsake stop going on about that child. The woman's the one with a gun at her throat.

Woman   Yes, but the child's the one who'll suffer.

Woman   By the way, is that what you meant by special police techniques? Because talk about technique. They're miles away. They're shitting themselves.

Man   The word I actually used was strategy.

Man   Strategy my arse.

Police (*from a distance*)   Drop your gun.

Woman   Fantastic.

Woman   Police to the rescue.

Man   Some strategy.

Man   You'll see – when they go in for the kill.

Woman   There's only one person I can see going in for the kill round here.

Man   It's practically a *fait accompli*, if you ask me.

Woman   That poor poor child.

Man   If you go on any longer about that poor poor child, you're going to get a smack in the face.

Man   D'you think this is really the moment to be arguing? Let's show a little dignity. We're witnessing a human tragedy. We're staring into the face of death.

Police (*from a distance*)   This is the police. Drop your gun. You are surrounded.

The onlookers burst out laughing.

Zucco   Tell her to give me the car-keys. It's a Porsche.

Lady   Idiot.

Woman   Give him the keys, give him the keys.

Lady   Absolutely not. He can get them himself.

Man   You're going to get your face blown right off, my darling.

Lady   Well thank god. At least I'll be spared the sight of *your* ugly faces. Thank God for that.

Woman   What an appalling woman.

Man   Nasty piece of work. There are so many cruel and unpleasant people in this world.

Woman   *Make* her hand them over. Surely one of you men can go through her pockets and find the keys?

Woman   Hey. You. If you suffered so much as a child. If the Germans stepped on your face and threatened your mother. Show us you've still got some balls – or one ball at least – even if it *is* small and shrivelled up.

Man   With all respect, you deserve a slap round the face. It's lucky for you I'm a gentleman.

Woman   Go through her pockets – get out the keys – *then* slap me round the face.

The **Man**, *trembling, goes up, reaches out, feels in the* **Lady**'s *pocket, and takes out the keys.*

Lady   Idiot.

The Man (*triumphantly*)   What about that then? What about that? Someone bring round the Porsche.

The **Lady** *laughs.*

Woman   She's laughing. How can she laugh when her child's about to die?

Woman   How horrible.

Man   She must be insane.

Man   Give the keys to the police. They can take care of that at least. I assume they know how to drive a car.

The **Man** *comes running back.*

Man   It's not a Porsche, it's a Mercedes.

Man   Which model?

Man   280 SE, I think. Beautiful machine.

Man   Mercedes make a nice car.

Woman   Whatever kind it is, just get it. Get it before he kills us all.

Zucco   I want a Porsche. I don't want people taking the piss.

Woman   Tell the police to find a Porsche. Don't argue with him. He's mad, totally mad. Just find him a Porsche.

Man: That's something they should be capable of at least.

Man   I wouldn't count on it. They'll still miles away.

Some of them head for the police.

Man   Look at us. We're just ordinary people and we've got more guts than they have.

Woman (*to the* **Child**)   You poor darling. Is that nasty foot hurting you?

Zucco   Shut up. No one talks to him. He's not to open his mouth. Come on – shut your eyes – don't move.

Man (*to the* **Lady**)   What about the mother? How are you feeling?

Lady   Fine, thank you, absolutely fine. But I'd be feeling a great deal happier if you kept your big mouths shut and all went back to your fitted kitchens and screaming shitty little brats.

Woman   She's got no feelings, no feelings at all.

Policeman (*from the other side of the crowd*)   Here are the car-keys. It's a Porsche. Over there. You can see it from here. (*To the crowd.*) Pass him the keys.

Man   *You* pass him the keys. Killers are your department.

Policeman   We have our reasons.

Woman   Reasons bollocks.

Man   I'm not touching those keys. It's not my job. I've got a wife and kids.

Zucco   I'll shoot the woman, then I'll put a bullet through my own head. I don't give a fuck about living. I don't give a fuck about anything, be*lieve* me. I've got six bullets. I'll kill five people – then I'll kill myself.

Woman   He means it, he means it. Let's get out of here.

Policeman   Don't move. You're making him nervous.

Man   You're making us nervous by doing sweet fuck-all.

Man   Just leave them to get on with it. There's a plan. There must be.

Policeman   Don't move.

He puts the keys on the ground and uses a stick to push them to **Zucco** *through the legs of the crowd.* **Zucco** *slowly bends down, picks up the keys, and puts them in his pocket.*

Zucco   I'm taking the woman with me. Out of my way.

Woman   The child's safe. Oh God, thank goodness.

Man   What about the woman though? What's going to happen to *her*?

Zucco   Out of my way.

Everyone moves back. Still holding the gun, **Zucco** *leans over, grabs the child by the hair, and shoots him in the back of the neck. People scream and run. With the gun to the woman's throat,* **Zucco** *heads for the car across the almost deserted park.*

XI   Le deal / It's a deal

Reception of the Little Chicago hotel.
The **Madam** *in her armchair, the* **Girl** *waiting.*

Girl   I'm ugly.

Madam   Don't be silly, duck.

Girl   I'm fat. I've got a double chin and a double stomach to go with it – breasts like footballs – and it's a good thing I can't see my backside because I know for a fact that with every step I take it seesaws up and down behind me like two legs of bacon.

Madam   Just shut it, you little fool.

Girl   I *know* it does, I *know* it does. Dogs follow me in the street with their tongues hanging out dribbling slobber. If I let them, they'd sink their teeth into me like meat on a slab.

Madam   Whatever gave you that idea, you daft little goose? You're pretty. You're well-rounded. And you've got a proper figure. D'you imagine a man appreciates some piece of dead twig he's frightened will snap off in his hands? Because what a man appreciates, my darling, is a nice round handful.

Girl   But I'd *like* to be thin. I'd *like* to be a piece of dead twig they were frightened of snapping.

Madam   Well *I* wouldn't. And besides just because you're fat today doesn't mean you won't be thin tomorrow. Women go through changes in their lives – it's not something to worry about. When I was a kid like you I was so thin you could almost see right through me – just a scrap of skin and a few bones. Not a breast in sight. As flat as a boy. Which made me pretty angry, since I wasn't too fond of boys in those days. I used to dream of a proper body, dream of having beautiful breasts. So I made myself some out of cardboard. But of course the boys found me out, and whenever they went past, they elbowed me in the chest and completely flattened them. Well after a few goes of that, I fixed a needle inside – and they screamed to high bloody heaven, believe you me. Then of course, things started filling out and fattening up, and I was a happy woman. So stop worrying, you daft little cuckoo: just because you're fat today doesn't mean you won't be thin tomorrow.

Girl   So what? Today I'm fat, ugly and miserable.

The **Brother** *enters, talking to a* **Pimp***. Neither pays any attention to the* **Girl***.*

Pimp (*impatiently*)   That's too much.

Brother   You can't *put* a price on it.

Pimp   Everything has a price – and yours is far too high.

Brother   But if you can put a price on something you're saying it can't be worth much. You're saying we can haggle, that the price can go up and down. Whereas what I've done is set an abstract price for something priceless. It's like a Picasso – have you ever seen someone say a Picasso's too expensive? Have you ever seen the owner drop the price of a Picasso? Because in situations like that the price is an abstraction.

Pimp   It may be an abstraction, but it's still one that goes from my pocket into yours. And I suppose the hole it makes in my pocket is an abstraction too?

Brother   A hole like that soon fills up. Believe me, you'll fill it up so fast you'll forget the price you paid in less time than the time you're taking to discuss it. Not that there's anything here to discuss. Take it or leave it. Make the best deal of the year or remain a poor man.

Pimp Don't get edgy, don't get edgy – I'm thinking.

Brother That's fine – you think – but don't take too much time. I'm going to have to take her back to her mother.

Pimp Okay. It's a deal.

Brother (*to* **Girl**) Your nose is shiny, chicken. How about putting some powder on it.

They watch her go out.

So . . . My Picasso?

Pimp I still say it's expensive.

Brother She'll make you so much money you won't remember what you paid for her.

The money changes hands.

Pimp When will she be available?

Brother Don't get edgy, don't get edgy – there's plenty of time.

Pimp No there is not 'plenty of time'. You've got the money, I want the girl.

Brother You've *got* the girl – or as good as.

Pimp Now you've got the money you're regretting it.

Brother I regret nothing, nothing at all. I'm thinking.

Pimp Thinking about what? This isn't the moment for thinking. I want to know when.

Brother Tomorrow, the day after tomorrow.

Pimp Why not today?

Brother Okay – why not today – why not tonight?

Pimp Why not right now?

Brother You're getting edgy, you're getting so fucking edgy.

*They hear the **Girl**'s footsteps.*

Brother Right now. Okay, it's a deal.

*The **Brother** rushes off and hides in one of the rooms. The **Girl** enters.*

Girl Where's my brother?

Pimp He's asked me to take care of you.

Girl I want to know where my brother is.

Pimp Listen, you're coming with me.

Girl I don't want to go with you.

Madam Just do exactly what you're told, you great fat turkey. A brother's orders are final.

*The **Girl** goes out with the **Pimp**. The **Brother** emerges from the room and sits opposite the **Madam**.*

Brother It wasn't my idea – I swear to you it wasn't. But she went on and on, on and on about coming here and going on the game. She's looking for someone – don't ask me who – but someone she has to find. She's sure she'll find him here. It was not my idea. No older brother ever watched over a sister the way I have. My chicken, my little darling, I've never loved anyone the way I've loved her. I can't help what's happened. We're just victims of evil. It was what she wanted – all I did was give in to her. I've never been able to say no to my baby sister. We're victims of evil and now it will never let us go. (*He cries.*)

Madam You piece of shit.

XII   La Gare / Railway Station

Zucco *and the* **Lady**.

Zucco   Roberto Zucco.

Lady   Why d'you keep saying your name all the time?

Zucco   I'm frightened I'll forget it.

Lady   People don't forget their names. Your name must be the last thing you forget.

Zucco   Not me. I'm forgetting mine. I can see it written inside my head, but less and less well, less and less clearly, as if it's fading. I have to peer closer and closer before I can read it. I'm frightened of ending up not knowing my name.

Lady   I won't forget it. I'll be your memory.

Zucco (*after a pause*)   I like women. I like them too much.

Lady   You can never like them too much.

Zucco   I love them, I love them all. There aren't enough women.

Lady   In which case you love me.

Zucco   Well of course. You're a woman.

Lady   Why have you brought me here?

Zucco   Because I'm going to catch a train.

Lady   What about the Porsche? Why don't you go off in the Porsche?

Zucco   I don't want to be noticed. In a train, nobody sees anyone.

Lady   And am I supposed to come with you?

Zucco   No.

Lady   Why not? There's no reason for me not to come. I took a liking to you the moment I saw you. I'm coming with

you. And besides, that's what you want – or you'd have killed
me by now or let me go.

Zucco   I need you to give me money for the train. I don't
have any. My mother was supposed to give me some but she
forgot.

Lady   Mothers always do. Where do you want to go?

Zucco   Venice.

Lady   Venice? What a peculiar idea.

Zucco   D'you know Venice?

Lady   Naturally. Everyone knows Venice.

Zucco   It's where I was born.

Lady   Congratulations. I always thought no one was born
in Venice, but everyone died there. The babies must be
born covered in dust and spiders' webs. At any rate, France
has certainly cleaned you up. I can't see one speck of
dust. This country is a wonderful detergent.
Congratulations.

Zucco   I have to get away from here. I absolutely have to get
away. I won't be caught. I won't be locked away. All these
people are scaring the shit out of me.

Lady   What? Be a man, can't you. You've got a gun – they'd
run a mile if you just took it out of your pocket.

Zucco   I'm shit-scared *because* I'm a man.

Lady   Well *I'm* not scared. After everything you've made me
go through I'm still not scared – and never have been.

Zucco   That's because you're not a man.

Lady   You're much too complicated.

Zucco   If they catch me, they'll lock me away. And if they
lock me away, I'll go insane. I'm *already* going insane. Police
everywhere. People everywhere. It's like being locked away
already. Don't look at them. Don't look at anyone.

Lady Do I really look like I'm going to give you away? Idiot. I could've done that a long time ago. These scum disgust me. Whereas you I rather like.

Zucco Just look at them all: all mad and full of hatred. All of them killers. I've never seen so many killers all at once. One flick of the switch and they'd start murdering each other. I don't understand why the switch doesn't flick right now – inside their brains. Because they're all primed to kill. Like laboratory rats. Like rats in a cage. They want to kill. You can see it in their eyes – in the way they walk – the way their fists are clenched in their pockets. I can spot a killer at a glance – their clothes are thick with blood. This place is full of them. We have to stay calm and not move. We have to avoid their eyes. They mustn't see us – we have to be transparent. Or otherwise – if we *do* look into their eyes, and they catch us looking, if they start to look back at us and stare, the switch in their heads will flick on and they'll kill and they'll kill. If just one of them starts, everyone here will murder everyone else. One flick of the switch is all it takes.

Lady Shut up. You're getting hysterical. I'll go and buy us both tickets. Just calm down or you're going to give us away. (*After a pause*) Why did you kill him?

Zucco Kill who?

Lady My son, you idiot.

Zucco Because he was a little prick.

Lady Who told you that?

Zucco You did. You told me he was a little prick. You told me he took you for a fool.

Lady And what if I *liked* being taken for a fool? What if I *liked* little pricks? What if I liked little pricks more than anything in the world – more than all the big bastards? What if little pricks were the only thing I *didn't* detest?

Zucco Then you should've told me.

Lady I *did* tell you, you idiot, I *did* tell you.

Zucco   Then you shouldn't've refused me the keys. You shouldn't've humiliated me. I didn't want to kill him, but after that business with the Porsche one thing simply led to another.

Lady   Liar. Nothing 'led' to anything – everything went wrong. *I* had the gun pointing at me, so why was *he* the one who had his head blown apart with blood everywhere?

Zucco   If it'd been your head, there would've been blood everywhere too.

Lady   But I wouldn't've had to see it – idiot – I wouldn't've had to see it.. I don't give a damn about *my* blood – it's nothing to with me. But his blood was everything to do with me – since I'm the one who damn well pumped it into his veins – it was mine – it was my affair – and my personal affairs are not something you splatter about – in a park – in front of a bunch of idiots. Now I've nothing left to call my own. Anyone could be stepping in the only thing that was really mine. And in the morning the gardeners will wash it away. What's left for me now – well? – what's left for me now?

Zucco *stands*.

Zucco   I'm going.

Lady   I'm coming with you.

Zucco   Stay where you are.

Lady   You don't even have the money for the train. You haven't even given me time to let you have it. You don't give anyone time to help you. You're like a flick-knife – open one moment – snapped shut and pocketed the next.

Zucco   I don't need anyone to help me.

Lady   Everyone needs someone to help them.

Zucco   Don't start crying. You look like a woman who's going to start crying. I hate that.

Lady   You told me you loved women. All of them. Even me.

Zucco   Except when they look like women who are going to start crying.

Lady I promise you I won't cry.

She starts to cry. **Zucco** *moves away.*

Lady What about your name, you idiot? Are you even capable of telling me what it is now? Who'll remember it for you? You've forgotten it already, I know you have. I'm the only one who remembers it now. You're leaving without your memory.

Zucco *goes. The* **Lady** *remains seated, watching the trains.*

XIII Ophélie / Ophelia

Same place. Night.
The station is deserted. The sound of rain.
The **Sister** *enters.*

Sister What have they done with my dove? What filth have they dragged her through? What vile cage have they locked her in? What twisted lecherous animals are stalking round her? I have to find you, my turtledove, and I'll keep on looking until it kills me.

Pause

Of all the disgusting animals on this earth the most disgusting is the human male. That smell they have revolts me. The smell of sewer rats, or pigs in muck. The stagnant smell of rotting corpses.

Pause

Men are filthy. They don't wash. They let the filth and revolting liquids they secrete build up on their unwashed bodies like a prize possession. Men can't smell each other because all men smell the same. That's why they go round together all the time – and why they visit prostitutes – because only prostitutes can tolerate the smell – for money. I washed that little child so many times. Bathed her before dinner, bathed her in the mornings, scrubbed her back and scrubbed her hands, scrubbed under her nails, washed her hair every day, cut her nails, washed her whole body every day with warm water and soap. I kept her pure and white, I preened her feathers like a turtledove. I protected her and kept her safe in a clean cage so as not to have her spotless whiteness spattered by the filth of this world, by the filthiness of men – so she would not be tainted by the tainted stench of men. And the rat of rats – the stinking pig, the degenerate male who sullied her, who hauled her through the mud and dragged her by the hair to his heap of filth – was her own brother. I should've killed him, I should've poisoned him, I should've stopped him stalking my turtledove's cage. I should've wrapped barbed wire round my truelove's cage. I should've stamped the rat dead and burned him in the stove.

Pause.

Everything here is filthy. This whole city is filthy and teeming with men. Let the rain fall and let it keep on falling, let it fall on that heap of filth and softly wash my little turtledove.

XIV   L'arrestation / The Arrest

Little Chicago.
Two **Police Officers**.
Prostitutes – and among them, the **Girl**.

First Officer   Seen anyone?

Second Officer   No. No one.

First Officer   It's ridiculous. This job is ridiculous. Stuck here like a couple of bollards. We might just as well be back on traffic duty.

Second Officer   It's perfectly logical. This is where he killed the inspector.

First Officer   Exactly: the one place he'll never come back to.

Second Officer   The murderer always returns to the scene of the crime.

First Officer   Come back here? What makes you think he'd do that? He didn't leave anything behind. Nothing – not even a suitcase. He's not crazy. We're just a couple of bollards with no *raison de* fucking *être*.

Second Officer   He'll be back.

First Officer   Instead of this we could be having a drink with *Madame*, chatting to the girls, or taking a little stroll somewhere with all these other calm, quiet individuals. Little Chicago must be the quietest place in town.

Second Officer   There's always fire beneath the ash.

First Officer   What fire? What ash? I can't see anything burning. Even the young ladies here are as calm and quiet as check-out girls. The clients stroll around as if it's a public park. And the pimps do their tours of inspection like bookshop assistants checking the books are safely on the shelves and nothing's been stolen. No, I can't see anything burning. Our friend won't be back, I'll bet you – I'll bet you a quick one at *Madame's*.

Second Officer   Well he definitely went back home after killing his father.

First Officer   Because he had stuff to do.

Second Officer   What stuff to do?

First Officer   Killing his mother. But once he'd done that, he never went back. And because he's got no more inspectors left to kill, he won't be back here either. I feel like an idiot. I can feel my arms and legs growing leaves and roots. I can feel myself sinking into the concrete. Come on: let's slip inside for a quick one. Everything's calm – everyone's taking their quiet little stroll. I mean can you really see anyone who looks like a killer?

Second Officer   Killers never do look like killers. Killers go for quiet little strolls in the crowd just like you and me.

First Officer   Then he must be mad.

Second Officer   A killer is mad by definition.

First Officer   Not necessarily, not necessarily. I can think of times when I've felt like killing people, if the truth be known.

Second Officer   Exactly – those are the times you nearly went mad.

First Officer   Very possibly, very possibly.

Second Officer   No question.

Zucco *enters.*

First Officer   But the fact is – even if I *was* mad – even if I *was* a killer – you'd still never catch me taking a quiet little stroll at the scene of my crime.

Second Officer   Look at that bloke.

First Officer   What bloke?

Second Officer   Bloke over there. Taking a quiet, so to speak, little stroll.

First Officer   Everyone here's taking a quiet little stroll. Little Chicago's turned into a public park. Next thing you know we'll get kiddies playing ball.

Second Officer   Bloke in the army fatigues.

First Officer   Yes, I can see.

Second Officer   Remind you of anyone?

First Officer   Very possibly, very possibly.

Second Officer   Might almost be *him*.

First Officer   Impossible.

Girl: (*sees* **Zucco**) Roberto.

She throws her arms round him and kisses him.

Second Officer   It's him.

First Officer   Absolutely no doubt about it.

Girl   I've looked and looked for you, Roberto – and I've betrayed you. I've cried and cried so much I've turned into a tiny island in the middle of a sea of tears, and now the last waves are drowning me. I've suffered so much my suffering could fill up the earth's chasms and flood out from its volcanoes. I want to stay with you, Roberto. I want to watch over every beat of your heart and every breath you take. I want to press my ear against you and hear the noise your body makes, tending to the workings of your body like a mechanic tending his machine. I'll keep all your secrets – I'll be your suitcase full of secrets – I'll be the bag where you store away your mysteries. I'll look after your weapons, and protect them from rust. You'll be my agent and my secret. And I'll be the suitcase you travel with – and the one who carries it – and the one who loves you.

First Officer (*going up to* **Zucco**)   Identify yourself.

Zucco   I'm the murderer of my father, my mother, a police inspector, and a child. I'm a killer.

The **Officers** *take him away.*

XV   Zucco au soleil / Zucco in the sun

The prison rooftops, noon.
Throughout the scene no one is visible, except **Zucco** *when he climbs to the top of the roof.*
We hear the mingled voices of prisoners and prison officers.

Voice   Roberto Zucco has escaped.

Voice   Again.

Voice   Who was guarding him?

Voice   Who was responsible?

Voice   We must look like fucking idiots.

Voice   You *do* look like fucking idiots.

Laughter.

Voice   No talking!

Voice   He must have accomplices.

Voice   He *doesn't* have accomplices. That's why he always manages to get away.

Voice   On his own.

Voice   On his own – like a hero.

Voice   We need to comb the corridors.

Voice   He's lying low somewhere.

Voice   He's curled up sweating in some little hole.

Voice   He won't be sweating because of *you* lot.

Voice   Zucco won't be sweating at all – he'll be laughing in your fucking faces.

Voice   Zucco's laughing in everyone's fucking face.

Voice   He won't get far.

Voice   This is a modern prison. Escape's not an option.

Voice   It's impossible.

Voice   Physically impossible.

Voice   Zucco's had it.

Voice   Zucco may've had it – but in the meantime he's climbing the roof and laughing in your fucking faces.

Zucco, *barefoot and bare-chested, reaches the top of the roof.*

Voice   What are you doing up there?

Voice   Come down immediately.

Laughter.

Voice   You've had it this time, Zucco.

Laughter.

Voice   Zucco – Zucco – tell us how you manage to never spend more than an hour in prison.

Voice   What's your secret?

Voice   Where did you slip out? Show us the way.

Zucco   Go upwards. Don't try and go over the walls, because beyond the walls, there are still more walls: prison goes on for ever. You can only escape from the rooftops, towards the sun. They'll never put a wall between the sun and the earth.

Voice   But what about the guards?

Zucco   The guards don't exist. Simply don't see them. And anyway, I could hold five of them in one hand and crush them in one go.

Voice   Where does your strength come from, Zucco? Where d'you get your strength?

Zucco   When I move, I charge. I don't see the obstacles – and because I don't see them, they vanish before me of their own accord. I'm strong and alone, I'm a rhinoceros.

Voice   But what about your mother and father, Zucco? It's wrong to harm your parents.

Zucco   It's normal to kill your parents.

Voice   But a child, Zucco – you shouldn't kill a child. It's your *enemies* you kill – people who can defend themselves. Not a child.

Zucco   I don't have enemies and I never attack. I crush other living creatures not because I'm evil but because I step on them without seeing them.

Voice   Have you got money – money stashed away somewhere?

Zucco   I've no money. Anywhere. I don't need money.

Voice   You're a hero, Zucco.

Voice   He's Goliath.

Voice   He's Samson.

Voice   Who's Samson?

Voice   A gangster from Marseilles.

Voice   I knew him in prison. A real animal. He could lay out ten men at a time.

Voice   Liar.

Voice   With his bare hands.

Voice   With the jawbone of an ass, actually. And he wasn't from Marseilles.

Voice   Some woman fucked him over.

Voice   I know. Delilah. The business with the hair.

Voice   There's always a woman who'll betray you.

Voice   If it wasn't for women we'd all be free.

The sun climbs higher, shining with extraordinary intensity. A great wind begins to blow.

Zucco   Look at the sun.

The courtyard becomes completely silent.

Zucco   Can't you see anything? Can't you see how it moves from side to side?

Voice   We can't see a thing.

Voice   The sun's hurting our eyes. It's dazzling us.

Zucco   But look what's coming out of it. The sun has an erection. That's where the wind's coming from.

Voice   The sun has a *what?* An *erection?*

Voice   Shut your faces!

Zucco   Move your head – see how it moves as you do.

Voice   How *what* moves? *I* can't see anything moving.

Voice   How can anything up there be moving? It's all been nailed and bolted into place since the beginning of time.

Zucco   It's the source of the wind.

Voice   We can't see anything any more. There's too much light.

Zucco   Turn to the east and it turns there too. Turn to the west and it follows you.

A hurricane begins to blow. **Zucco** *sways.*

Voice   He's mad. He's going to fall.

Voice   Stop it, Zucco – you're going to smash yourself to pieces.

Voice   He's mad.

Voice   He's going to fall.

The sun rises higher, with the blinding brilliance of an atomic explosion. Nothing else can be seen.

Voice (*shouts out*)   He's falling!

ENDNOTES

Koltès and Succo

Bernard-Marie Koltès first 'encounter' with the criminal who
was to inspire the central character of his play took place at
the beginning of 1988 in the Paris metro. A wanted poster
showed four photos of Roberto Succo. Each photo was of a
face so different that you had to look several times to know
they were all of the same boy. Koltès was struck by these
pictures, by the beauty of the changeable face which they
showed. Some time later, on a TV news programme, he saw
an extract from his 'performance' on the roof of the prison at
Treviso – arrested the previous day, Roberto Succo had
managed to get away from his guards for a moment during an
exercise break, jumping up on to a small shed which he then
used to climb up onto the roof. For more than an hour he
spoke to the journalists who had assembled outside the prison,
threw roof-tiles at the warders' cars and started taking his
clothes off. The entertainment continued with Succo hanging
from an electrical cable. From which he subsequently fell.

What touched Koltès in these images was again the
attractiveness of the boy, and the purely theatrical dimension
which this scene contained. So he began writing, having read
a few press cuttings. As for me, I was already working on the
story of the real Succo. I suggested to Koltès that we meet. He
was very keen to do so. We spent a long afternoon discussing
our shared passion. Obviously we were embarked on very
different journeys – whilst I was trying with the obstinacy of
an ant to reconstruct Succo's real story, Koltès had completely
absorbed his character. What was uncanny was that he had
arrived at an extraordinary intuitive understanding of Succo,
and had drawn psychological conclusions which were pretty
close to the truth. So using very different methods we had still
managed to reach similar conclusions. But as for the darkness
of Succo, the thing which made him unique as a killer, his
complete coldness about the crimes he had committed, the
terrible madness which sometimes possessed him, the
incarnation of absolute evil which he represented – I don't
think Koltès was interested in these things. Fundamentally it
didn't really matter to him that he was a killer. He was

fascinated to the point of identification. Perhaps he was already beyond such monstrousness.

We saw each other again and I gave him some more information. I told him how the young girl who finally helped to identify Succo had at first thought his name was 'Juce'. And that she had subsequently remembered that 'Succo' meant '[fruit] juice' in Italian, which had confused her. The press, who at that point weren't aware of this particular story, had sometimes referred to him as 'Succo' and sometimes 'Zucco'. Koltès took notes on little scraps of paper. I passed on to him several other similar details, and played him a recording supposedly of Succo's voice, in which he said 'To be or not to be . . . that is the question. I believe that . . . there are no words, there is nothing to say [. . .] So one year, a hundred years, it's all the same . . . sooner or later we all have to die. All of us. And that . . . that's what makes the birds sing, the birds. That's what makes the bees sing. That's what makes the birds laugh.'

Because of Koltès' illness I thought twice about letting him hear this desperate monologue. But it was a sort of confirmation of the character he had sensed was there. When he heard it he was very moved. Not long afterwards he sent me the play, with a little note attached to it in which he mentioned how important this document had been to him. Indeed, he had included a part of it in Scene Eight, which he had titled 'Just before dying'. Koltès also said that at the time of sending me the play he found himself 'between two great journeys'. I wanted to call him to talk about the play. He was already dead.

Pascale Froment
author of '*Je te tue, histoire vraie de Roberto Succo,*
assassin sans raison' © Gallimard

Koltès on 'Roberto Zucco'

An improbable journey, a mythical character, a hero like Samson or Goliath, monstrously strong, finally laid low by a stone or a woman.

Preface to '*Dans la solitude des champs de coton*'

A *deal* is a commercial transaction between purchaser and provider involving prohibited or strictly controlled items of exchange conducted in neutral indeterminate spaces not intended for such use by means of tacit understanding recognised signals or conversation with double meaning – the aim of which is to avoid the risk of betrayal and fraud implicit in such operations – at any hour of day or night independently of the official opening hours of authorised commercial outlets but mostly when the latter are shut.

From *Pour mettre en scène 'Quai ouest'*

Think of all language as ironic [. . .]

Never try and work out a character's psychology from what he/she says, but on the contrary, make the character speak his/her lines as a function of what you deduce them to be from their *actions*. [. . .]

Love, passion, tenderness – or whatever – should be left to go their own sweet way. To give them too much attention always means diminishing them and making them look ridiculous.

From '*Un hangar, à l'ouest*'

Theatre

I tend to see a stage as a temporary place, which the characters are always thinking about leaving. It's like the place where you set yourself this problem: this isn't real life, how do we get out of here? The solutions always seem to have to happen offstage, a bit like in the classical theatre. [. . .]

I've always rather hated theatre, because it's the opposite of life; but I always come back to it and love it because it's the only place where you can say that this isn't life.

Writers

I think directors produce far too many plays from the
repertoire. A director thinks himself heroic if he directs a new
play in between six plays by Shakespeare or Chekhov or
Marivaux or Brecht. It simply isn't true that writers who've
been dead for one or two or three hundred years tell stories
about now. Of course you can find parallels – but I'm afraid
no one's going to persuade me there's anything contemporary
about Lisette and Harlequin and their amorous intrigues. The
language of love is now quite different – so it's *not* the same
thing. How would we react if contemporary writers started
writing plays about servants and countesses conducting
intrigues in eighteenth century *chateaux*? I'm the first to admire
Chekhov, Shakespeare, Marivaux, and to try and learn from
them. But even if our age doesn't include writers of that
quality, I think it's better to put on a living writer, with all
their faults, than ten Shakespeares.

Mozart existed, we still listen to him and that's a good
thing. That doesn't stop even more people listening to Billie
Holiday or Marvin Gaye or Michael Jackson, and that's a very
good thing. No sensible person would dream of comparing
one with the other, of saying that there are no Mozarts around
today and finding soul music contemptible.

No one, especially not theatre directors, has the right to say
that there are no playwrights. Of course we don't know who
they are because we don't put their plays on, and it's
considered almost unheard of today to have your work
produced in good conditions – when actually this is the
simplest of things to do. How do you expect writers to get
better if nothing is asked of them and no one tries to get the
best out of what they've done. The writers of our age are as
good as the directors of our age.

From John Freeman's 'Face to Face' interview with Carl Jung

Is there any one case that you can now look back on and feel that perhaps it was the turning point in your thought?

Oh yes, I had quite a number of experiences of that sort, and I went even to Washington to study Negroes at the Psychiatric clinic there, in order to find out whether they have the same type of dreams as we have, and these experiences and others led me then to the hypothesis that there is an impersonal stratum in our psyche, and I can tell you an example. We had a patient in the ward; he was quiet but completely dissociated, a schizophrenic, and he was in the clinic or the ward twenty years. He had come into the clinic as a matter of fact a young man, a little clerk and with no particular education, and once I came into the ward and he was obviously excited and called to me, took me by the lapel of my coat, and led me to the window, and said: 'Doctor! Now! Now you will see. Now look at it. Look up at the sun and see how it moves. See, you must move your head, too, like this, and then you will see the phallus of the sun, and you know, that's the origin of the wind. And you see how the sun moves as you move your head, from one side to the other!' Of course, I did not understand it at all. I thought oh, there you are, he's just crazy. But that case remained in my mind, and four years later came across a paper written by the German historian, Dieterich, who had dealt with the so-called Mithras Liturgy, a part of the Great Parisian Magic Papyrus. And there he produced part of the so-called Mithras Liturgy, namely it had said there: 'After the second prayer you will see how the disc of the sun unfolds, and you will see hanging down from it the tube, the origin of the wind, and when you move your face to the regions of the east it will move there, and if you move your face to the regions of the west it will follow you.' And instantly I knew – now this is it! This is the vision of my patient!

But how could you be sure that the patient wasn't unconsciously recalling something that somebody had told him?

Oh, no. Quite out of the question, because that thing was

not known. It was in a magic papyrus in Paris, and it wasn't even published. It was only published four years later, after I had observed it with my patient.

And this you felt proved that there was an unconscious which was something more than personal?

Oh well, that was not a proof to me, but it was a hint, and I took the hint.

Methuen Contemporary Dramatists
include

Peter Barnes (three volumes)
Sebastian Barry
Edward Bond (six volumes)
Howard Brenton
  (two volumes)
Richard Cameron
Jim Cartwright
Caryl Churchill (two volumes)
Sarah Daniels (two volumes)
David Edgar (three volumes)
Dario Fo (two volumes)
Michael Frayn (two volumes)
Peter Handke
Jonathan Harvey
Declan Hughes
Terry Johnson
Bernard-Marie Koltès
Doug Lucie

David Mamet (three volumes)
Anthony Minghella
  (two volumes)
Tom Murphy (four volumes)
Phyllis Nagy
Philip Osment
Louise Page
Stephen Poliakoff
  (three volumes)
Christina Reid
Philip Ridley
Willy Russell
Ntozake Shange
Sam Shepard (two volumes)
David Storey (three volumes)
Sue Townsend
Michel Vinaver (two volumes)
Michael Wilcox